Bundle Up!

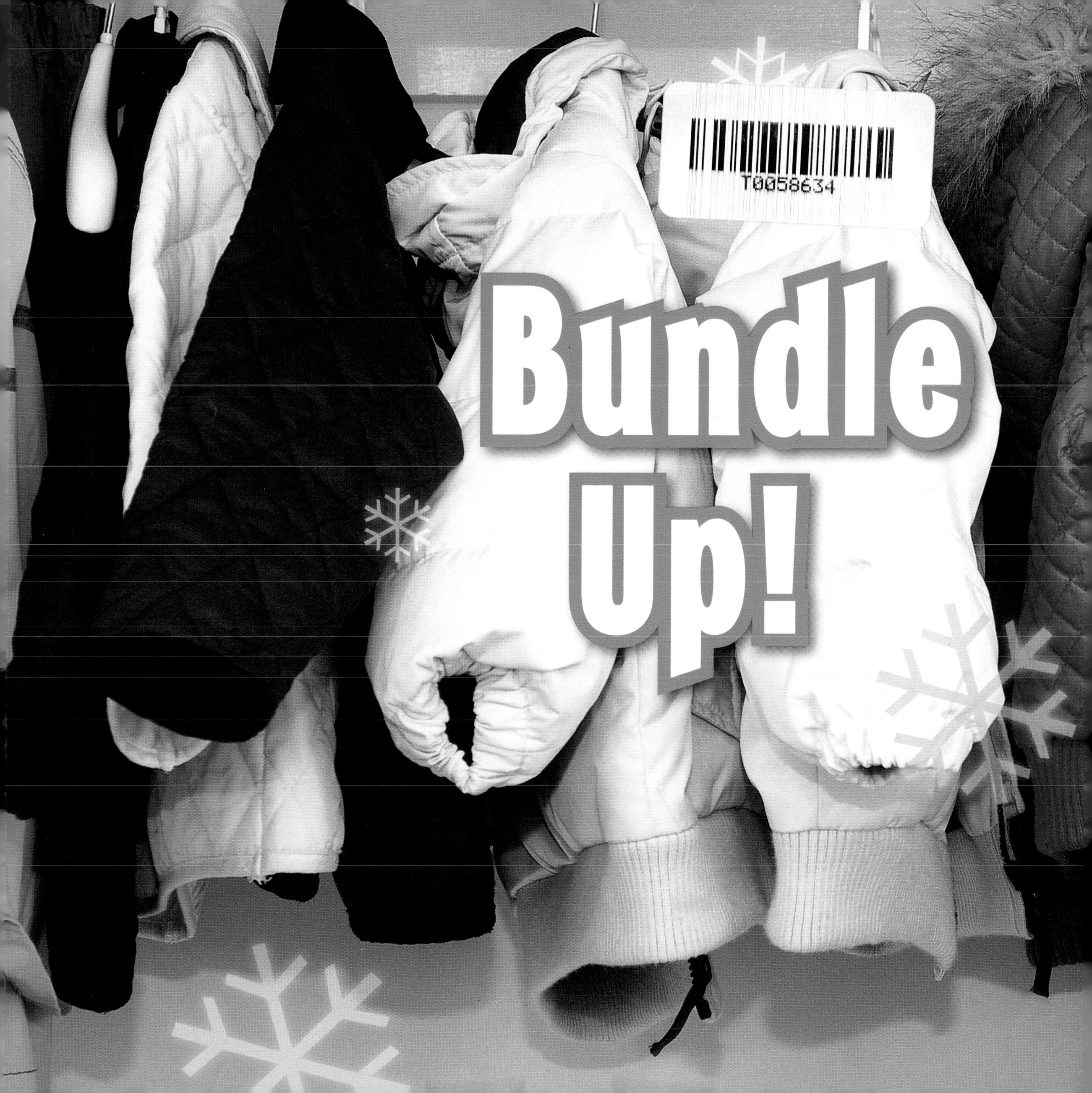

T0058634

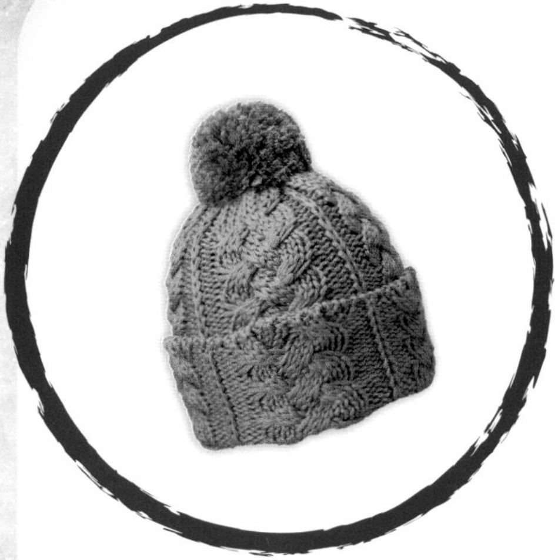

hat

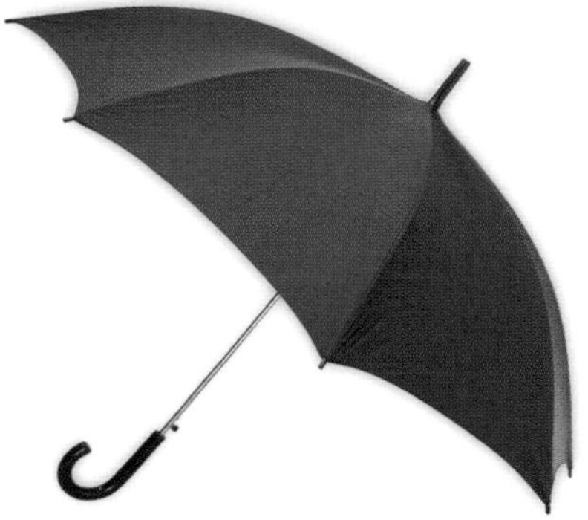

umbrella

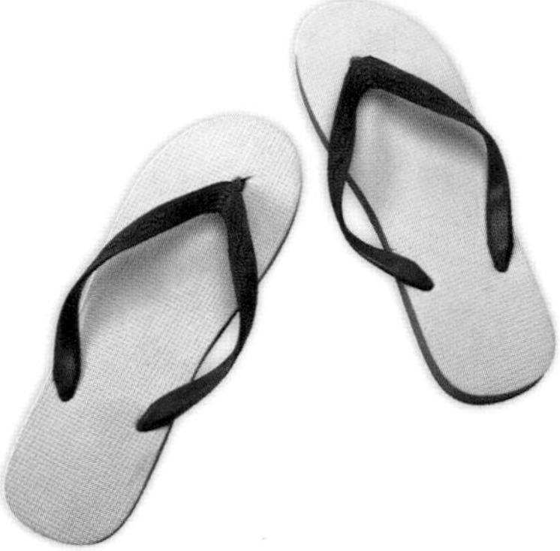

sandals

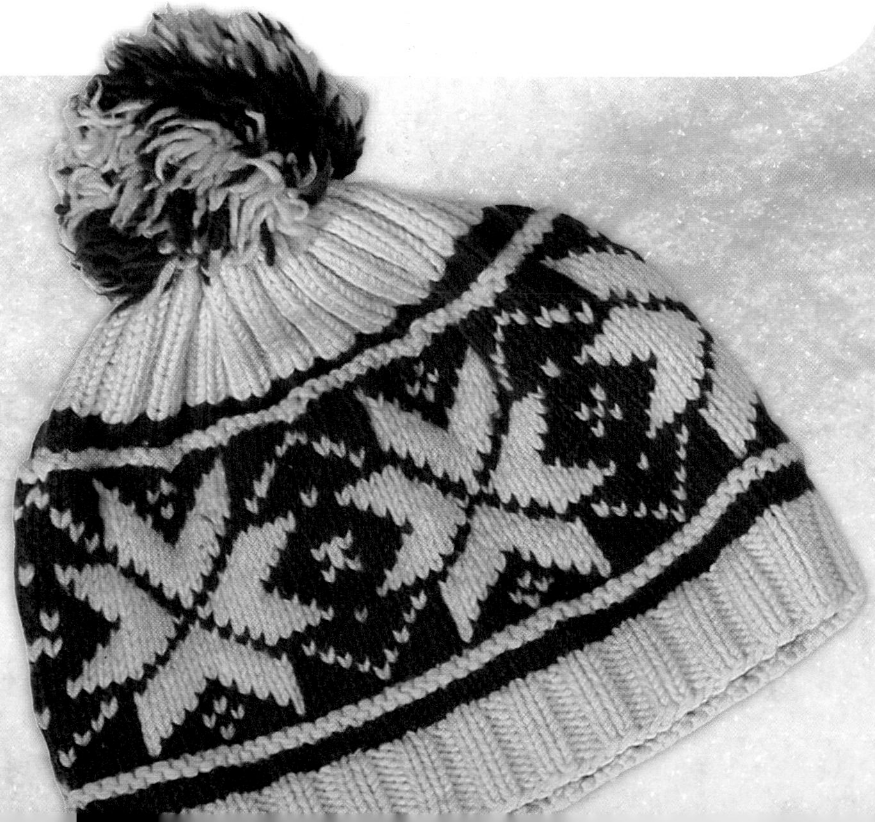

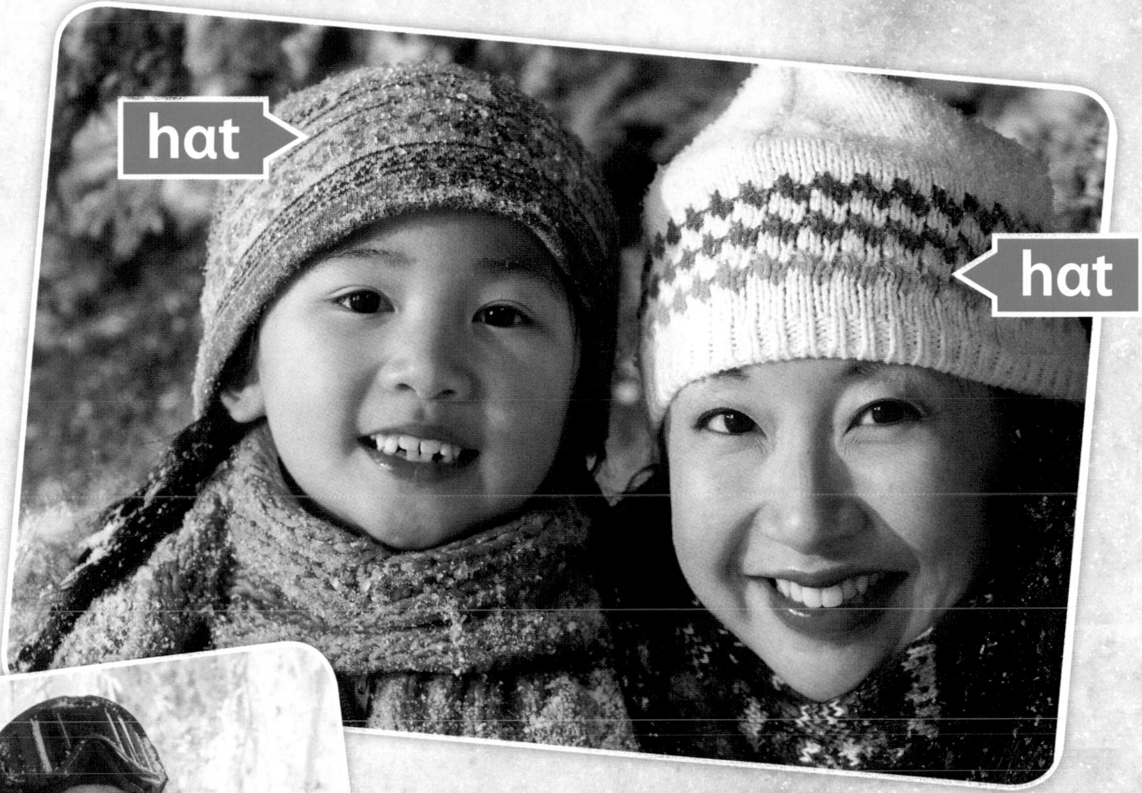
hat
hat

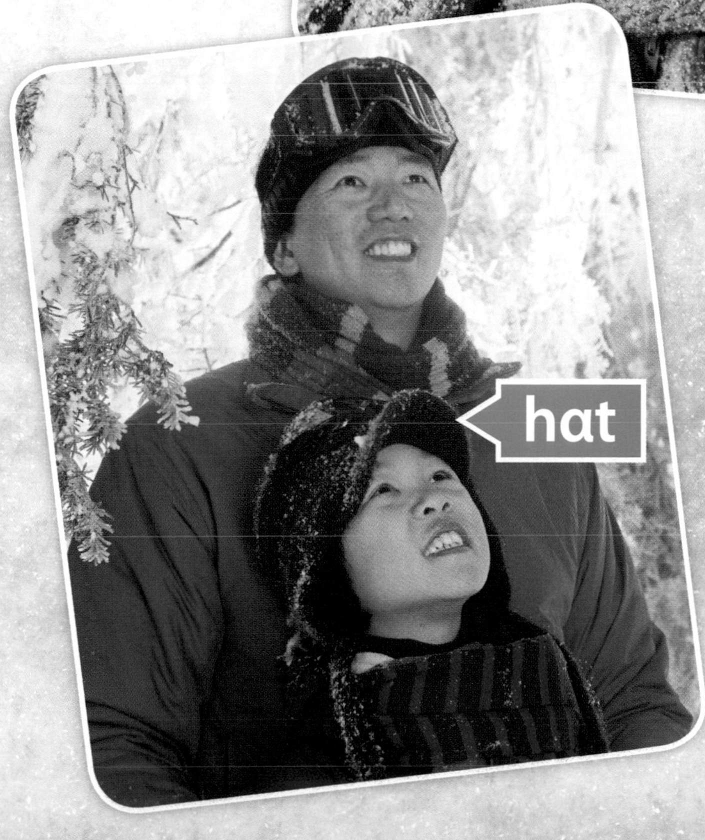
hat

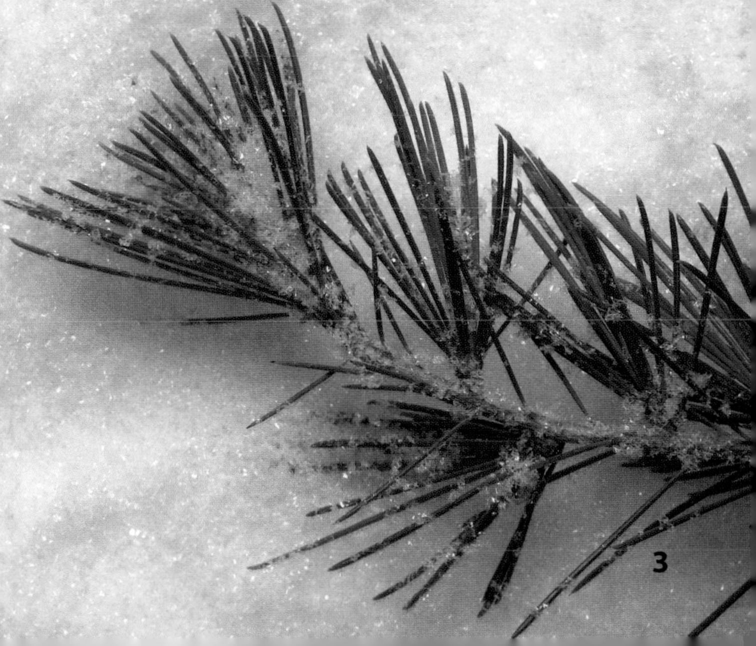

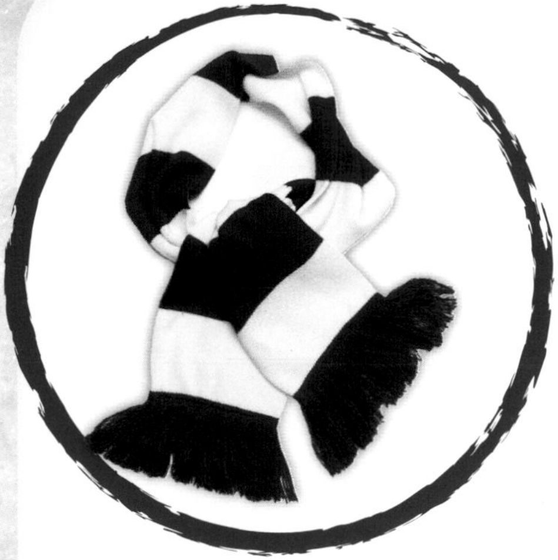

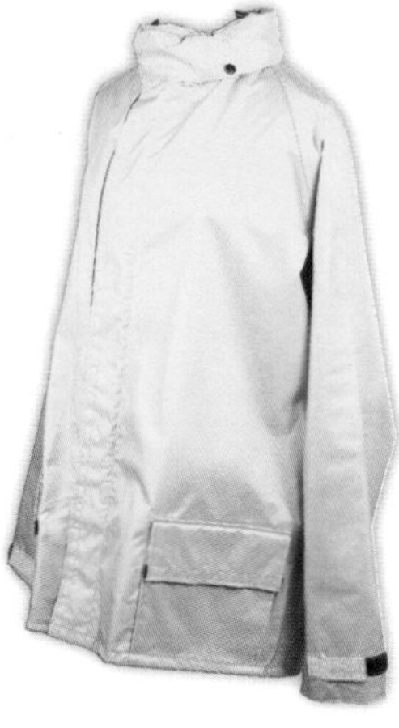

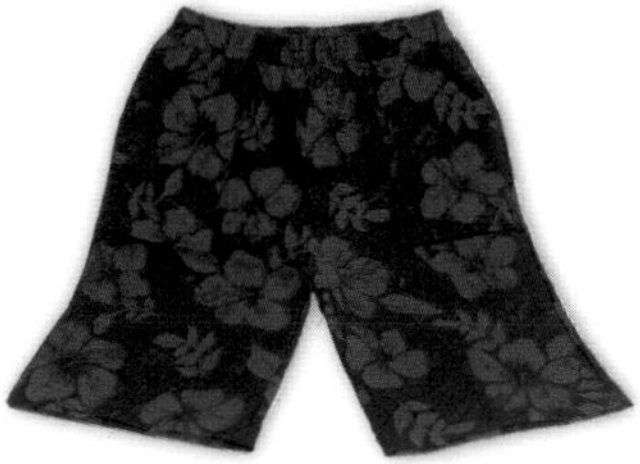

scarf raincoat shorts

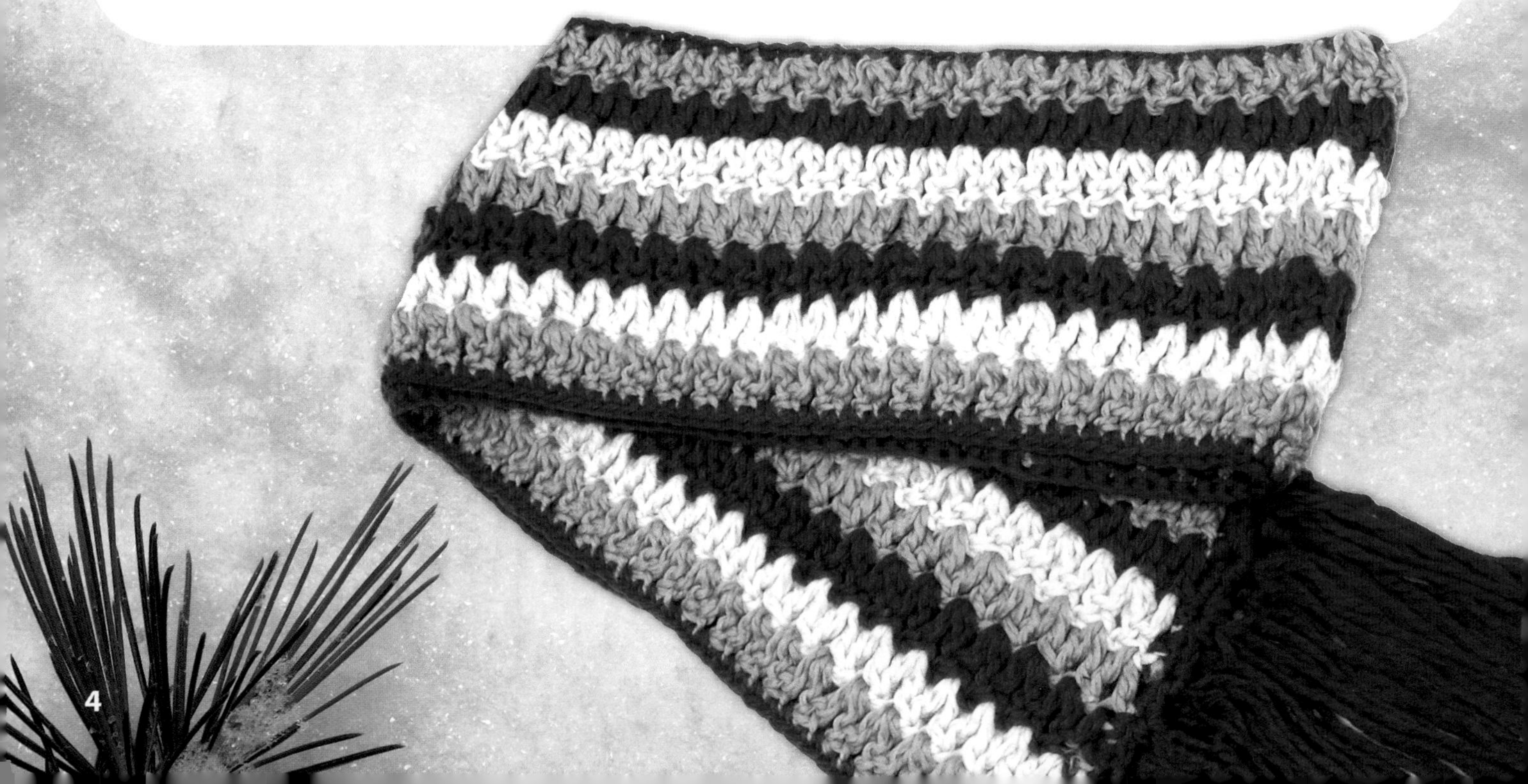

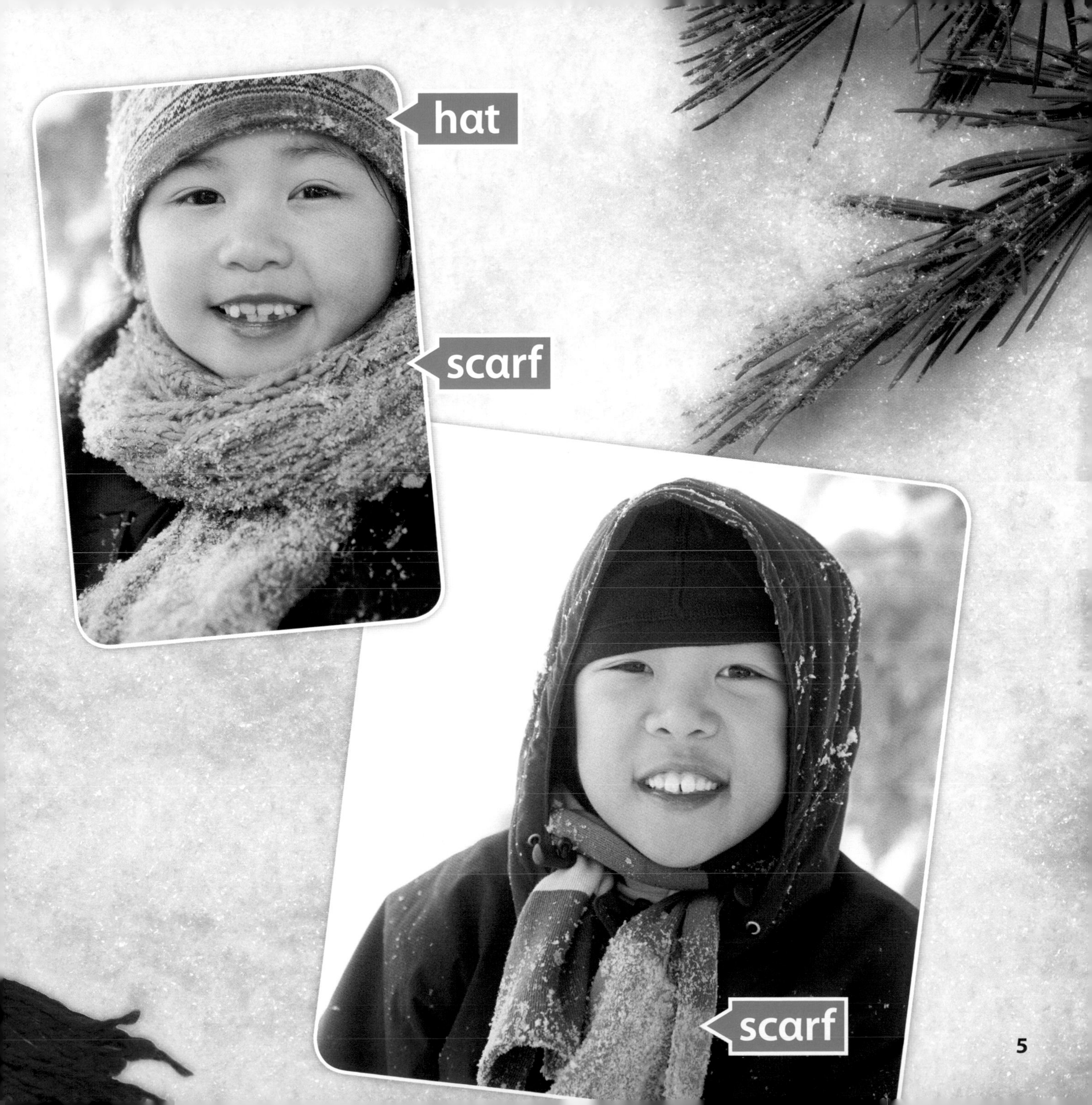
hat
scarf
scarf

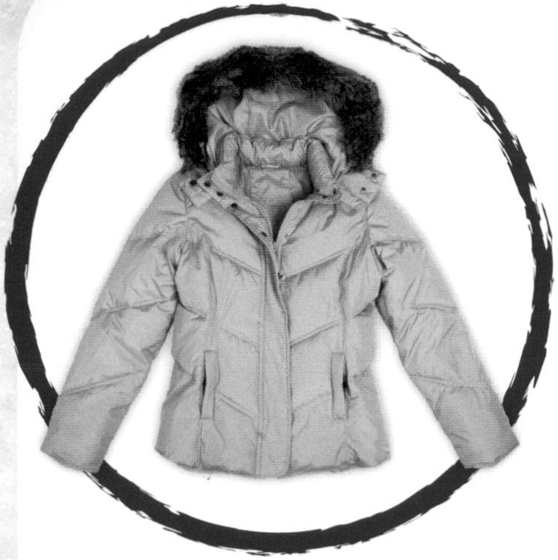

coat

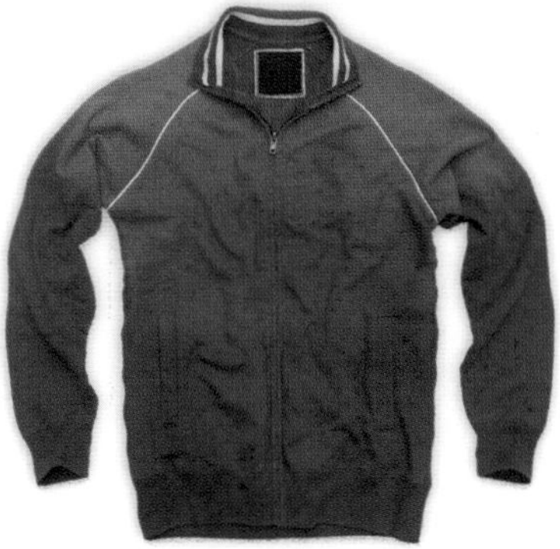

jacket

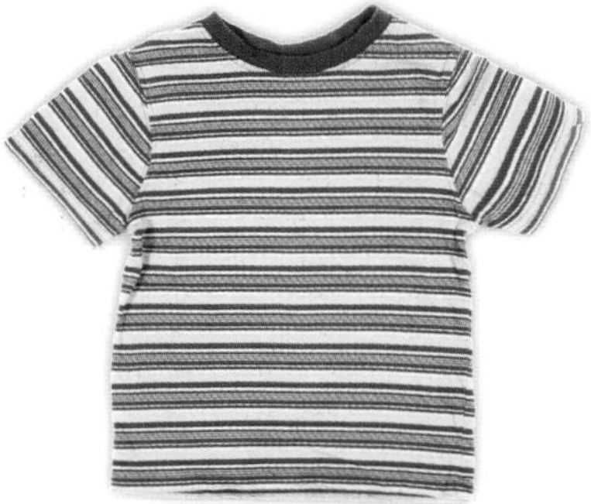

shirt

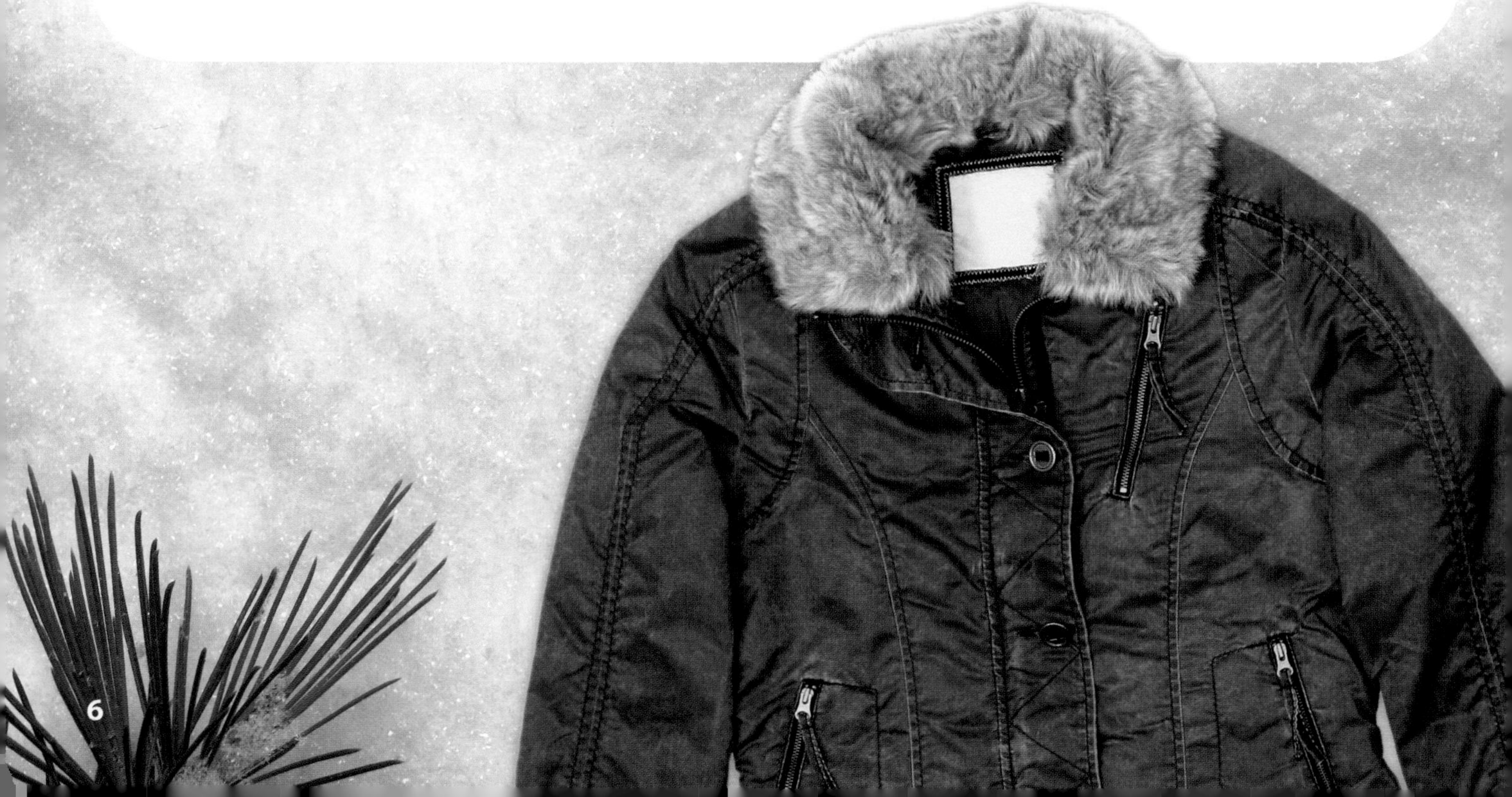

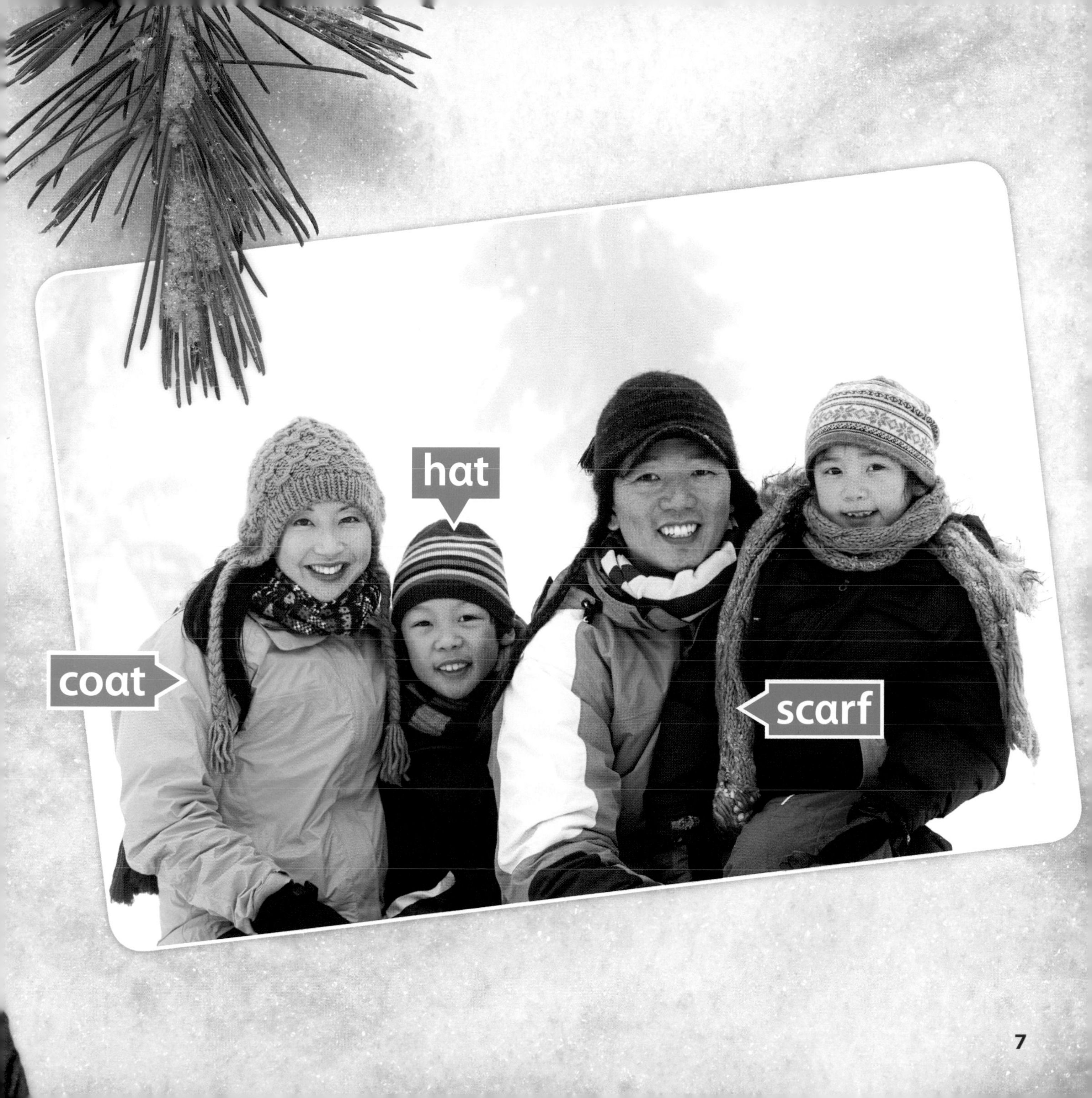
hat
coat
scarf

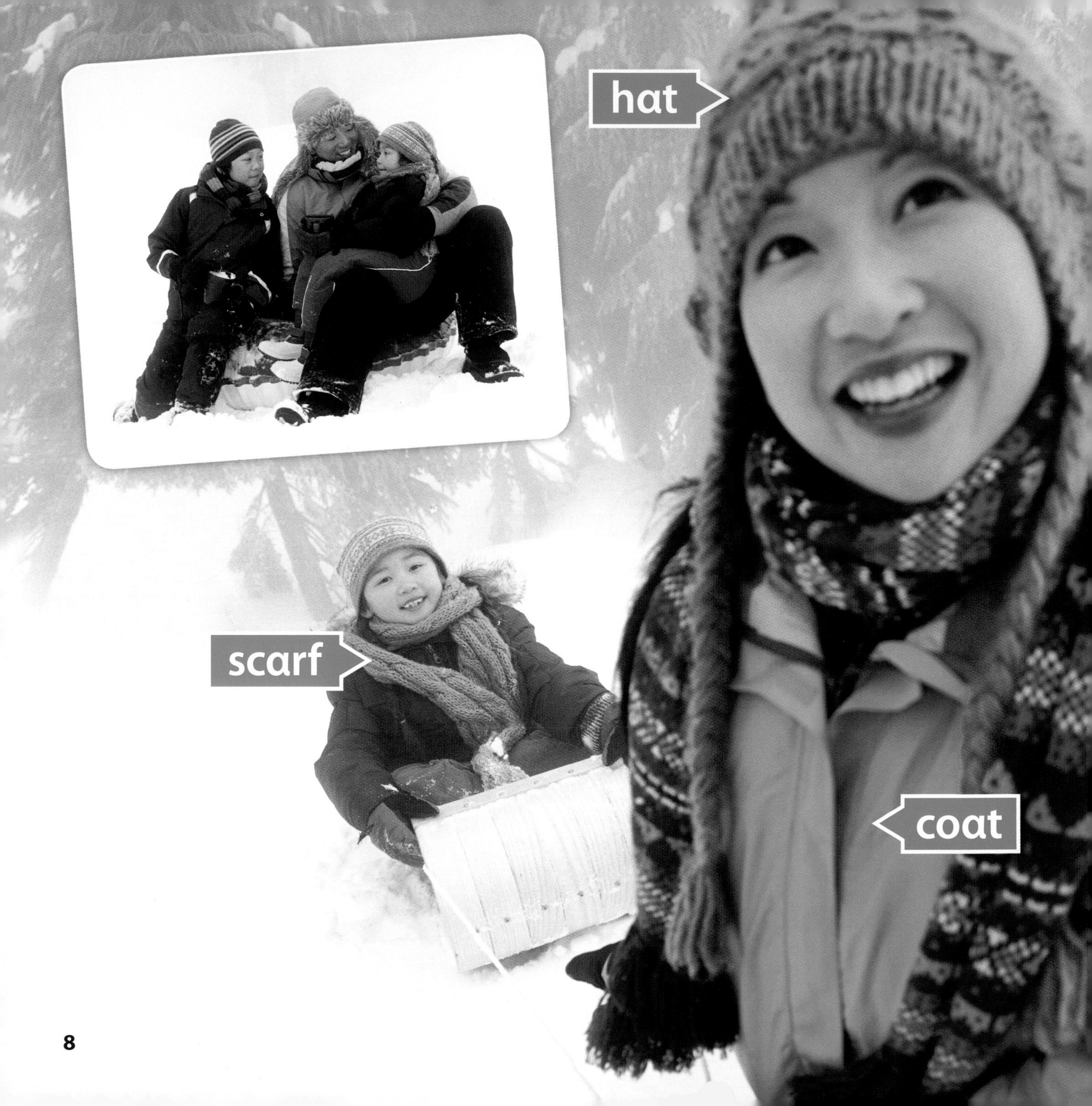
hat
scarf
coat